HIP-HOP

50 Cent

Ashanti

Beyoncé

Mary J. Blige

Chris Brown

Mariah Carey

Sean "Diddy" Combs

Dr. Dre

Missy Elliott

Eminem

Hip-Hop: A Short History

Jay-Z

Alicia Keys

LL Cool J

Ludacris

Nelly

Notorious B.I.G.

Queen Latifah

Reverend Run (Run-D.M.C.)

Will Smith

Snoop Dogg

Tupac

Usher

Kanye West

Pharrell Williams

Dr. Dre

Hal Marcovitz

Mason Crest Publishers

Dr. Dre

FRONTIS The innovative rapper and producer Dr. Dre remains an important figure in the world of hip-hop music.

PRODUCED BY 21ST CENTURY PUBLISHING AND COMMUNICATIONS, INC.

MASON CREST PUBLISHERS INC.
370 Reed Road
Broomall, Pennsylvania 19008
(866)MCP-BOOK (toll free)
www.masoncrest.com

Printed in Malaysia.

First Printing

9 8 7 6 5 4 3 2 1

Library of Congress Cataloging-in-Publication Data

Marcovitz, Hal.
Dr. Dre / Hal Marcovitz.
p. cm. — (Hip-hop)
Includes bibliographical references (p.) and index.
ISBN-13: 978-1-4222-0116-9 (hc)
ISBN-10: 1-4222-0116-3 (hc)
1. Dr. Dre, 1965– —Juvenile literature. 2. Rap musicians—United States—Biography—Juvenile literature. I. Title. II. Series.
ML3930.D7M37 2006
782.421649092—dc22
[B] 2006011443

Publisher's notes:

- All quotations in this book come from original sources, and contain the spelling and grammatical inconsistencies of the original text.
- The Web sites mentioned in this book were active at the time of publication. The publisher is not responsible for Web sites that have changed their addresses or discontinued operation since the date of publication. The publisher will review and update the Web site addresses each time the book is reprinted.

Contents

Hip-Hop Timeline

1970s Hip-hop as a cultural movement begins in the Bronx, New York City.

1970s DJ Kool Herc pioneers the use of breaks, isolations, and repeats using two turntables.

1970s Break dancing emerges at parties and in public places in New York City.

1970s Graffiti artist Vic pioneers tagging on subway trains in New York City.

1974 Hip-hop pioneer Afrika Bambaataa organizes the Universal Zulu Nation.

1976 Grandmaster Flash & the Furious Five pioneer hip-hop MCing and freestyle battles.

1979 The Sugarhill Gang's song "Rapper's Delight" is the first hip-hop single to go gold.

1982 Afrika Bambaataa embarks on the first European hip-hop tour.

1984 *Graffiti Rock*, the first hip-hop television program, premieres.

1985 *Krush Groove*, a hip-hop film about Def Jam Recordings, is released featuring Run-D.M.C., Kurtis Blow, LL Cool J, and the Beastie Boys.

1986 Run-D.M.C. are the first rappers to appear on the cover of *Rolling Stone* magazine.

1986 Beastie Boys' album *Licensed to Ill* is released and becomes the best-selling rap album of the 1980s.

1988 *Yo! MTV Raps* premieres on MTV.

1988 Hip-hop music annual record sales reaches $100 million.

1970 1980 1988

1989 DJ Jazzy Jeff & The Fresh Prince become the first hip-hop artists to win a Grammy Award.
1989 Rap is added as a new category to the *Billboard* charts.
1989 First gangsta rap album, *Straight Outta Compton*, is released by N.W.A.
1990s Hip-hop emerges in Europe.
1992 Dr. Dre's album *The Chronic* is released; it redefines West Coast rap.
1993 Rapper Snoop Dogg's album *Doggystyle* is the first debut album to hit the music charts at number one.
1996 West Coast rapper Tupac Shakur is shot and killed.
1997 East Coast rapper Notorious B.I.G. (aka Biggie Smalls) is murdered.
1989
2000
2006
2001 The hip-hop political action group, Hip-Hop Summit Action Network, is founded by Russell Simmons.
2003 Rapper Eminem becomes the first hip-hop artist to win an Academy Award.
2004 First National Hip-Hop Political Convention is held in Newark, New Jersey.
2005 Hip-hop artist Kanye West appears on the cover of *Time* magazine.
2005 Rapper Will Smith opens the Philadelphia Live 8 concert as part of 10 simultaneous concerts held worldwide to bring attention to the extreme poverty in Africa.
2006 Queen Latifah becomes the first hip-hop artist to receive a star on the Hollywood Walk of Fame.
2006 The Smithsonian Institute National Museum of American History announces the creation of a new hip-hop exhibition scheduled to open in three to five years.

Since the late 1980s, Dr. Dre has been one of the most popular and influential producers of rap music. In addition to creating his own successful albums, Dre has helped launch the careers of many of hip-hop's biggest stars.

1

An Influential Producer

By the late 1990s, rapper and record producer Dr. Dre had been on top of the hip-hop world for more than a decade. In 1996 Dre had established his own label, Aftermath Entertainment. He was always on the lookout for new voices in rap who could provide the label's fans with unique, cutting-edge sounds.

Starting with his days as a member of the rap group N.W.A, Dre was known for setting the standard in the **genre** of music known as "gangsta rap"—a style of hip-hop that celebrates crime, violence, and drug use. Under Dre's guidance, gangsta rappers had made hip-hop history, producing tough, gritty rhymes that captured the essence of life on the streets. Dre was always looking for new ways to tell the gangsta story.

One night in 1998, Dre stopped by the home of a friend, Jimmy Iovine, an executive for Interscope Records. Dre and Iovine often listened to demos of unknown artists together. According to a VH1 interview, when

Iovine asked Dre to give his opinion on a particular tape, Dre immediately liked the fiery hostility of the **lyrics** and beat. "He finds ways to rhyme words that don't seem like they should rhyme. I felt that," Dre told VH1. "There was a song called 'Bonnie and Clyde' that I really loved. . . . I knew I had to work with [that artist] right then."

Dre learned that the demo had been recorded by Marshall Mathers, an unknown rapper from Detroit who performed under the name Eminem. Dre believed Eminem's sound truly captured the restless attitude of **urban** young people. Since its inception in the 1970s, hip-hop music had always been regarded as the sound of young urban blacks. VH1 asked Dr. Dre what he thought when he discovered that Eminem was white. "Then my wheels started turning," the rap producer said. "I thought he would be able to get away with saying a lot more than I would get away with saying. If a black guy said that stuff, people would turn the radio off."

White rap artists had been successful, but none reached the degree of stardom enjoyed by the top black stars. Some, like Vanilla Ice, were considered corny, especially by those interested in the hardcore sound of gangsta rap. Dre was intrigued by the notion of a white rapper who would appeal to both white and black hip-hop fans.

Dre quickly signed Eminem to a contract. Their collaboration resulted in Eminem's first two albums: *The Slim Shady LP* and *The Marshall Mathers LP*. Both albums became big sellers as well as critical successes. Eminem would later tell *VH1*, "It was an honor to hear the words out of Dre's mouth that he liked my [music]. Growing up, I was one of the biggest fans of N.W.A., from putting on the sunglasses and looking in the mirror, and lip-synching to wanting to be Dr. Dre. . . . This is the biggest hip-hop producer ever."

Meet Slim Shady

Eminem's first two albums were very controversial. *The Slim Shady LP* introduced audiences to Eminem's dark side in the form of a character he called "Slim Shady." According to the album's biggest hit, "My Name Is," Slim is an angry trash-talking youth with no future. He drinks, takes drugs, abuses his family, and isn't afraid to lash out with his fists.

The Marshall Mathers LP contained lyrics that were homophobic and promoted violence against women. Gay rights groups were especially critical of the album. The lyrics on *The Marshall Mathers LP* contained more than a dozen hostile references to gays. In an interview

In 1998, Dr. Dre was impressed when he heard a demo tape by an unknown white rapper who performed under the name Eminem. Dre signed Eminem to his Aftermath Entertainment label, and produced his first two albums.

with *The Advocate*, a magazine that reports news in the gay community, activist Romaine Patterson said:

> **"While I love free speech, it does not really entitle us to make money or to be given a platform to be hurtful to other people. With kids in particular, in reference to Eminem, these words are becoming acceptable to them and are then going out of their mouths as quickly as they go in their ears, in the school hallways, in the locker rooms, on the street. Unfortunately, it has an impact on the lives of their peers, especially the gay and lesbian peers that are already struggling with low self-esteem."**

Dre dismissed the criticism, claiming that the lyrics were meant to be humorous and make people with such prejudices look silly. Eminem further defended his lyrics by explaining that they were written from the point of view of the Slim Shady character, a deplorable person made all the more distasteful by his hatred for gays. In a *Rolling Stone* interview, Dre told writer Anthony Bozza that the people complaining about the album's homophobia were merely jealous of its success. He said:

> **"I haven't really paid attention to the feedback; I've been in the studio doing my thing. But I'm not going to go and make it worse by speaking on it again. If people are really that offended by it, we should stop doing it and go on to a different topic. All in all, we just thought it was funny when we were making it up. I think people felt comfortable bringing it up because Em has gotten so big. A lot of these people probably don't care; they just want TV time. . . . It just goes to show you: If it's big, they're going to talk about it. . . . They were singling Eminem out. A lot of people love him, and right now a lot of parents think that he has their children's future in the palm of his hand."**

Despite the criticism, *The Marshall Mathers LP* became one of the most successful albums of 2000, selling more than 8 million copies. In

Eminem and Dr. Dre perform together at a 2000 concert in Seattle. When Eminem's first two albums were criticized for lyrics that seemed to advocate violence toward women and gays, Dre supported the controversial rapper.

2001, it was nominated for four Grammy Awards, including Album of the Year, which is the top award offered by the National Academy of Recording Arts and Sciences.

Tearing Down Walls

As the Grammy Awards show neared, resentment among gays intensified. Gay rights groups announced they would stage protests outside the awards theater in Los Angeles. Critics predicted that *The Marshall Mathers LP* would be passed over for Album of the Year. In the newspaper *Newsday*, music reporter Letta Tayler wrote that while there was no question that Eminem's album was cutting-edge hip-hop:

> **"It's one thing to nominate a rapper whom many listeners brand misogynist, homophobic, and obsessed with violence for the Grammy's top honor. It's quite another thing, even if the album for which he's nominated has sold 8 million copies, to let him win."**

Eminem tried to assure critics that he was not homophobic. He even agreed to perform a duet at the Grammys show with gay pop star Elton John. In an interview with reporters, John said, "I know I'm

Famed singer Elton John performed with Eminem at the 2001 Grammy Awards. By performing with the Rock 'n' Roll Hall of Fame singer, who is gay, Eminem hoped to prove to fans that he has no bias against homosexuals, despite his controversial lyrics.

going to get a lot of flak from various people, but I'd rather tear down walls between people than build them up. If I thought for one minute that he was hateful, I wouldn't do it."

The Marshall Mathers LP won three Grammy Awards that night: Best Rap Soloist for Eminem, Best Rap Duo or Group for Eminem and Dr. Dre (who also rapped on the album), and Best Rap Album. However, as critics predicted, the record was passed over for Album of the Year, which instead went to the more mainstream rock album *Two Against Nature* by Steely Dan.

Dr. Dre told TV entertainment news show *Access Hollywood* that he felt the Grammy voters were not prepared to present the top award to an album with such controversial lyrics. "To be perfectly honest, I think we were robbed," Dre said. "It was probably something the Grammys had to do because of the backlash they were going to get for giving [Eminem] the award."

Growing up in the ghetto of Compton, Andre Young saw firsthand the many problems that plague urban neighborhoods: high crime, gang violence, homelessness, and drug abuse. As a performer, he would straightforwardly discuss the things he saw on the streets.

2

Compton DJ

Andre Young, who would one day be known to his fans as Dr. Dre, was born February 18, 1965, in Compton, California. Compton was a suburb of Los Angeles that had deteriorated from a working-class community into a depressed neighborhood where drug abuse and gang violence were common. Andre's mother, Verna, was 16 years old when her son was born.

Verna was married briefly to Andre's father, Theodore Young, but it was a troubled relationship. Theodore was an abusive husband and a drug dealer. Eventually, Verna left, taking the couple's baby with her. She found a job as an office clerk and raised Andre on her own.

Verna Griffin recalled that her son had a gift for words, even when he was young. Andre's grandmother enjoyed reciting poetry to the boy, who quickly committed the words to memory. He also exhibited a love for music, even as a baby. In her biography, *Privileged to Live*, Verna recalled:

> **"It seems that he was born with a love for music. When I look back on his life, I think he began to develop this love when he was only a few months old. That was when I first noticed the soothing effect that music had on him."**

By age four, Andre knew how to work his mother's **turntable**, and he always volunteered to spin records during his mother's parties. Verna was a fan of rhythm and blues. She owned records by James Brown, Aretha Franklin, Martha and the Vandellas, and similar stars, and this was the music Andre first learned to appreciate. "Mom was 16 when I was born, so we grew up together and we like the same things," Dre told *Newsweek*. "I was the music man for her parties. I've always known what good music was."

Verna eventually remarried and had more children. Andre grew up with eight brothers and sisters.

"Wheels of Steel"

As Andre grew older, Verna couldn't help but notice that some of his friends never seemed to lack money. She suspected that they sold drugs. She said:

> **"I was worried more than anything that Andre would be drawn to the glitter of what drug money could buy. I often told him, 'Fast money is not good money.' I warned him about the kinds of people it brings and the discomfort it causes from having to look over your shoulder and constantly watch your back. I explained that it was better to live with legal income that trickles in slowly than to deal with the madness that fast money brings, including the possibility of being killed."**

In Compton, such a possibility was very real. The city was a dangerous place filled with notorious gangs. Many gang members were crack dealers or murderers. Members of one gang, who wore blue

Privileged To Live

Verna Griffin

A Mother's Story of Survival

Verna Griffin, Dr. Dre's mother, wrote a book in which she described her family's experiences in Compton and her son Andre's early life. *Privileged to Live: A Mother's Story of Survival* was published in 2005.

bandanas, called themselves the Crips. The gang earned its name from a news story in which victims reported being beaten by young men carrying walking canes, as though they were crippled. The Crips were involved in a long-standing rivalry with another gang called the Bloods. Andre promised his mother he would stay out of both gangs, and he made good on that promise.

As a teenager, Andre enrolled in Centennial High School in Compton. However, his studies suffered because he was constantly distracted by music. He had acquired two turntables, an amplifier, and a **music mixer**. As he spun the two silver turntables to create interesting beats and sounds, he sometimes referred to them as his "steel wheels." Andre's mother recalled how her son loved to play music loudly, which she endured because she knew if she could hear the music, then Andre and his brothers and sisters were home instead of getting in trouble elsewhere in the neighborhood.

By the time Andre was in high school, rap music was starting to attract a widespread audience. During the evenings, he would sneak into Los Angeles nightclubs to listen to the early rap acts. He became a big fan and soon began earning extra money working as a DJ at parties under the stage name Dr. Dre. According to one story, Andre took the name because his favorite basketball star was Julius "Dr. J" Erving. Another source says that he used to wear surgeon's masks while he worked at parties because it gave him an air of mystery.

Andre also found work as a DJ at the Los Angeles nightclub Eve After Dark, earning $50 a night. His talents became so much in demand that he dropped out of high school to work full time. He told *Rolling Stone*:

"When I was older, and I DJ'ed at Eve After Dark, I would put together this mix shelf, lots of oldies, Martha and the Vandellas and stuff like that, and when normally you go to a club and the DJs play all the hit records back to back, I used to put on a serious show. People would come from everywhere, just to see Dr. Dre on the wheels of steel."

The Birth of N.W.A

With his days free, Andre formed an **electro hop** group with some friends. They called themselves World Class Wrecking Cru. They

A young boy peers into an abandoned apartment in Compton used by drug addicts as a place to get high. Since the late 1970s the California city, with a population of about 93,000, has been considered a blighted, high-crime area.

dressed extravagantly, wearing tight Spandex jumpsuits, shirts with frilly collars, and capes. They found some **gigs** performing in small clubs in Los Angeles but failed to win a record deal. On his own, though, Andre recorded a single titled "Dr. Dre's Surgery," which he paid to have recorded. The single was sold in Compton stores and on street corners. Andre had no money for a fancy marketing campaign, but some 50,000 copies of the record were sold entirely through word-of-mouth. People who heard and enjoyed "Dr. Dre's Surgery" were soon encouraging their friends to buy a copy.

At around the same time Andre's single was becoming an underground hit, another Compton rapper named Eric Wright, who performed under the name Eazy-E, started his own record label. Eazy-E wanted his label, Ruthless Records, to concentrate on a new genre of hip-hop that was just being introduced on **ghetto** streets:

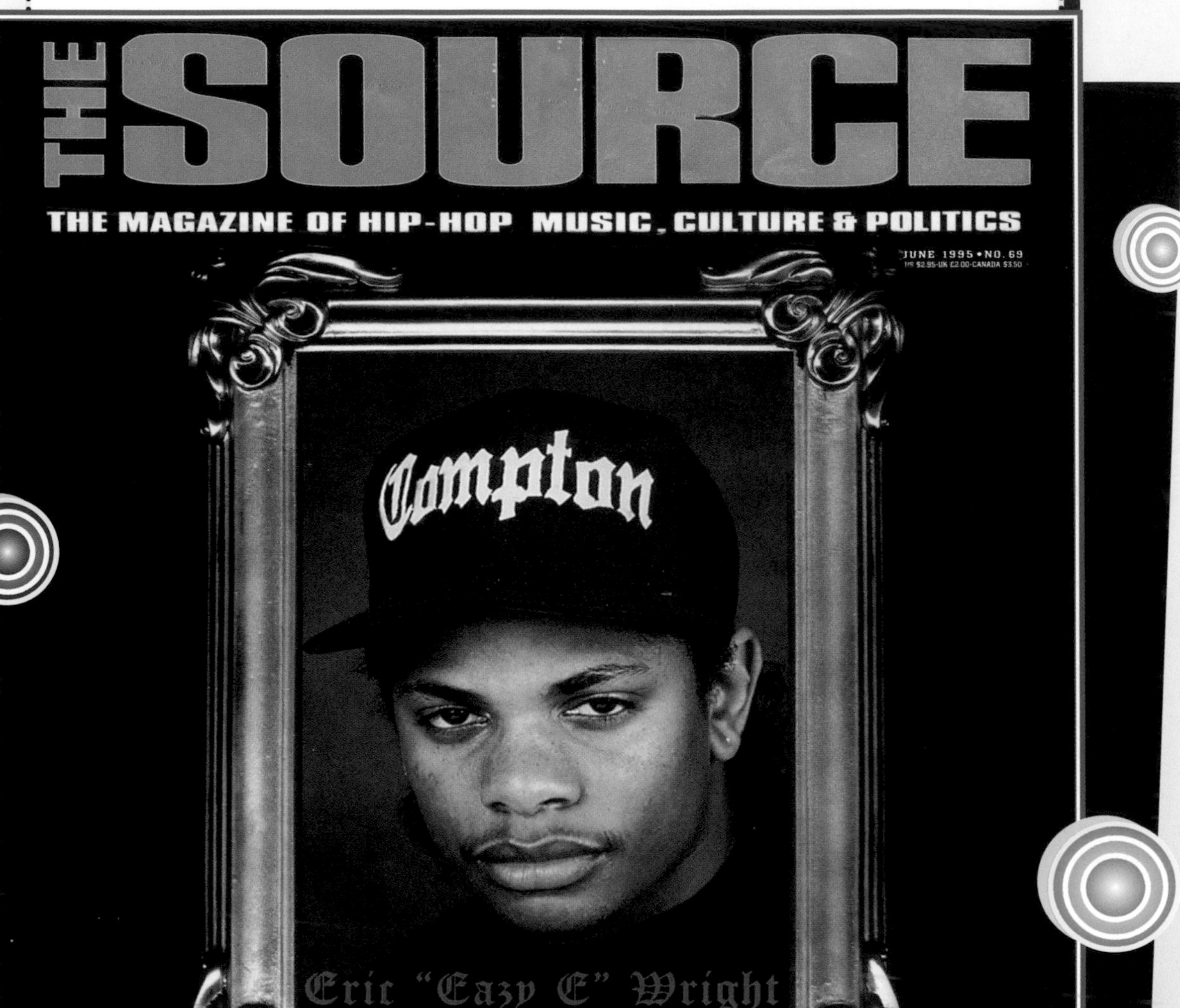

The influential rapper Eazy-E is pictured on a magazine cover shortly after his death in 1995. Eazy-E invited Dr. Dre to join the group N.W.A in 1986; together, they helped transform gangsta rap from an underground phenomenon into a mainstream music style.

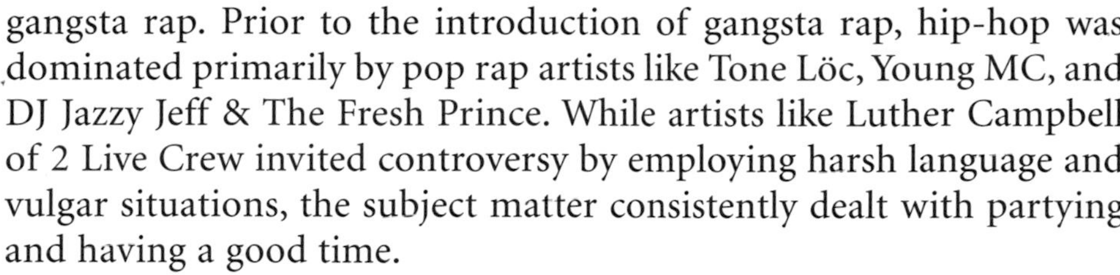

gangsta rap. Prior to the introduction of gangsta rap, hip-hop was dominated primarily by pop rap artists like Tone Löc, Young MC, and DJ Jazzy Jeff & The Fresh Prince. While artists like Luther Campbell of 2 Live Crew invited controversy by employing harsh language and vulgar situations, the subject matter consistently dealt with partying and having a good time.

In 1986, Eazy-E invited Andre to form a new rap group with DJ Yella, Arabian Prince, and Ice Cube. (MC Ren and The D.O.C. joined later when Ice Cube left for a year.) They called their new group N.W.A—Niggaz With Attitude.

The group's first album, released in 1987, was titled *N.W.A and the Posse.* Containing songs like "Panic Zone," "Fat Girl," "Dopeman," and "Tuffest Man Alive," it was essentially a record of party tunes, not unlike the rap songs that mainstream hip-hop artists were producing. The album was commercially successful. *N.W.A and the Posse* sold more than 500,000 copies, making it what the music industry calls a gold record.

But Dr. Dre, Eazy-E, and the other members of the group were not satisfied. N.W.A wanted to tell the true story of life in Compton, without trying to gloss it over. At night, gunfights between rival gang members were common. Drug deals went down on street corners. The police were a constant presence that bred fear among many young blacks; even those who were innocent felt like suspects. Soon after *N.W.A and the Posse* was released, the group members began working on a new album they believed would tell what life was really like for urban blacks in the United States. When that album hit the hip-hop scene in 1989, it was so controversial and cutting edge that it forever changed the direction of rap music.

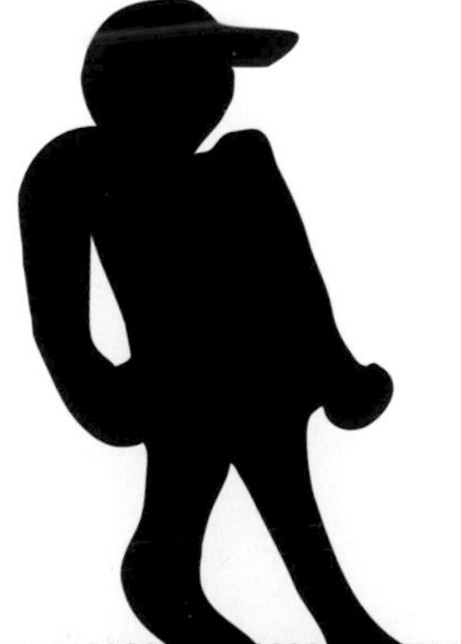

In his music, Dr. Dre wanted to present the unvarnished, hard-hitting stories of life in urban neighborhoods. Some critics praised the music for its realistic, gritty depiction of the problems and issues faced by many African Americans.

3

Songs for the Neighborhood

N.W.A's album *Straight Outta Compton* is today considered a classic that revolutionized the genre known as gangsta rap. However, when it was released in 1989, the album immediately drew criticism. One song, titled "F--- Tha Police," was particularly controversial because its lyrics encouraged and justified the use of violence against police officers.

Throughout the country, government leaders and law enforcement officials denounced the song's message. In a letter to Ruthless Records, an FBI official named Milt Ahlerich wrote:

"Advocating violence and assault is wrong, and we in the law enforcement community take exception to such action. . . . Law enforcement officers dedicate their lives

to the protection of our citizens, and recordings such as the one from N.W.A are both discouraging and degrading to these brave, dedicated officers.”

In Boston, an attorney named Jack Thompson led a campaign to ban sales of the album in record stores. He contended that the lyrics violated **obscenity** laws. Thompson's efforts were unsuccessful, however. The U.S. Constitution guarantees freedom of expression, meaning that no matter how offensive the lyrics may be to some people, creative artists still have a right to express themselves.

Triple Platinum

The tracks on *Straight Outta Compton* were not the first rap songs to be considered offensive. However, such hardcore rap albums often did not sell well. Radio stations usually refused to play the songs because the Federal Communications Commission, a government agency that regulates the airwaves, prohibits broadcasts of obscene material. To promote sales, gangsta rappers had to rely on word-of-mouth and live performances. But the furor over *Straight Outta Compton* resulted in national publicity for N.W.A. The attention helped the album go **triple platinum**, selling over 3 million copies. *Straight Outta Compton* became the first rap album to sell so many copies without radio support.

Despite the criticism, there were those who stood up for N.W.A. Jon Pareles, a music critic for the *New York Times*, wrote that while the group's songs may be “foul-mouthed,” the lyrics addressed true problems. Pareles said that other musicians, as well as writers and filmmakers, have long portrayed some police officers as corrupt and prone to violence. He wrote that the group's songs are “part of a long tradition of literature and art that doesn't respect authority; N.W.A is hardly the first to take the gangsters' side.”

In 1990, Ruthless Records released *100 Miles and Runnin'*, a shorter album of songs by N.W.A that did not include Ice Cube. Featuring Dr. Dre's slick production, the album was a moderate success and earned gold record status. The group's next major effort was 1991's *Efil4zaggin* (“Niggaz 4 Life” spelled backwards). This album was a big seller. It debuted at number two on the *Billboard* magazine charts and then quickly moved up to number one. Again, Dr. Dre's production attracted critical praise, although many of the songs on *Efil4zaggin* advocated violence, particularly toward women.

Like *Straight Outta Compton, Efil4zaggin* was the target of censorship and a campaign by Jack Thompson to ban the album. Government officials said they shared Thompson's concerns. In Minnesota, Attorney General Hubert H. Humphrey III sent a letter to the Minneapolis-based Musicland Group asking the company to withdraw the album from the 1,000 stores it operates in the United States. The company

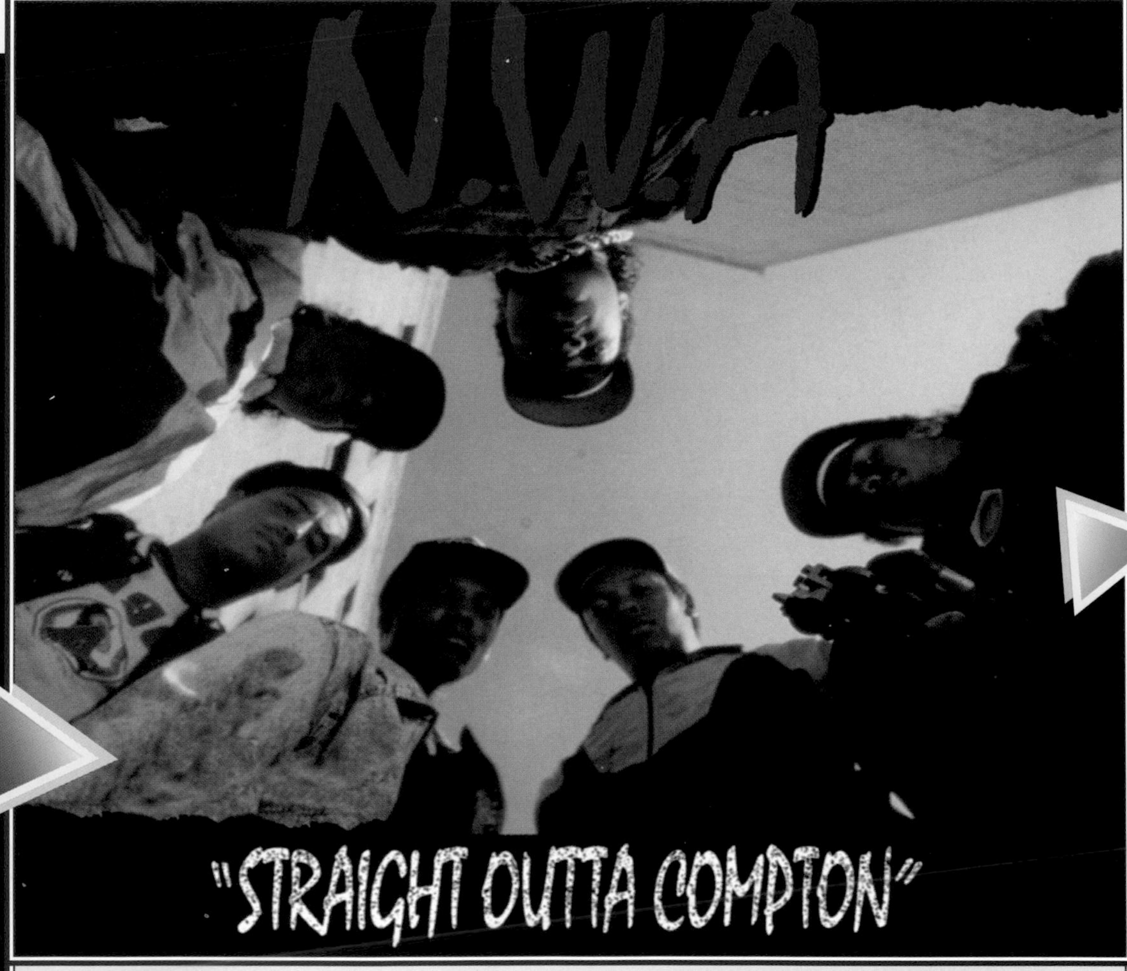

The cover of *Straight Outta Compton*, N.W.A's controversial 1989 album. Although radio stations refused to play songs from the album, public outrage over the explicit lyrics fueled a wave of publicity that helped *Straight Outta Compton* sell millions of copies.

refused, but a Musicland spokesman said the company had instructed its stores to refuse to sell the album to anyone under the age of 18. Many Musicland stores ignored the company's orders, though. A clerk at one of the company's stores in Cambridge, Massachusetts, told the *Boston Herald*, "We are supposed to ask [minors] if they have their parents' permission to buy it, but I don't ask because I believe that in the United States anyone should be able to buy anything they want."

Hard Partier

As with *Straight Outta Compton*, the national attention generated by the controversy over *Efil4zaggin*'s song lyrics helped make the album into a top-selling record. This made all the members of N.W.A very wealthy. Dre used his money to buy a mansion and a fleet of expensive cars. He also used his money on extravagant parties. He told *The Guardian* of London, England:

> **"You could come over on Sunday morning and there's just people laying out on the floor asleep. Girls all over the place. I was spending money on a lot of cars, jewelry, apartments all over town. I probably bought somewhere between eight to ten cars. Ferraris, I don't know how many Mercedes, Corvettes. . . . It was dumb. . . . I blew a lot of money."**

Dr. Dre was living the gangsta life he often rapped about. He was smoking marijuana, drinking, and finding it hard to control his temper—activities that soon got him in trouble with the law. In 1991, Dre was charged with assaulting a TV host in a nightclub after she aired a show that was critical of his music. He was sentenced to **probation** and was sued by the host for damages in the amount of several hundred thousand dollars.

A year later, the rap star pled guilty to assaulting a police officer in New Orleans, during a brawl that was sparked when he was refused admission to a crowded hotel lobby. A court sentenced him to 30 days house arrest. Also in 1992, he punched a record producer in the jaw, was again charged with assault, and again placed on house arrest. A year later, he was arrested for drunk driving, which was a violation of his probation on a previous assault charge. The judge sent him to jail for five months.

Dr. Dre contributed slick production to the successful N.W.A albums *100 Miles and Runnin'* (1990) and *Efil4zaggin* (1991). However, the producer, feeling unappreciated for his work, decided to leave Ruthless Records and form his own label.

Molding the Sound

In addition to promoting N.W.A's albums, Ruthless Records was also churning out records for other rappers. Dre did much of the production work on the label's releases. Although he rapped on N.W.A's records and occasionally appeared on the albums of other rappers, his real talent was in molding the sound—picking the beats and other background sounds, coordinating the voices of the rappers, judging how fast or slow to record the music, and deciding how soft or loud to make the raps and beats. For each song on each album, it was a tremendous undertaking to put all the pieces of the puzzle together, and Dre had a true talent for the craft.

In 1990, Marion "Suge" Knight and Dr. Dre agreed to form a new hip-hop label, Death Row Records. Knight had a reputation as a dangerous and ruthless man, and he surrounded himself with thugs and convicts.

Rolling Stone reporter Jonathan Gold wrote about watching Dre at work in the studio:

> **"Listening to a Dre beat take shape in the studio is like watching a snowball roll downhill in a Bugs Bunny cartoon, taking on mass as it goes. Dre may find something he likes from an old drum break, loop it and gradually replace each part with a better tom-tom sound, [or] a kick-drum sound he adores."**

The problem was that Dre did not think his talent was appreciated at Ruthless Records. He produced seven rap albums for Ruthless that went platinum, but argued constantly with Eazy-E over payment for his services. Dre joked in an interview with *Rolling Stone* that he was so strapped for cash he considered moving back in with his mother.

In 1990, Dre met Marion "Suge" Knight, who was working as a promoter for rap shows at nightclubs in Los Angeles. Knight, a former professional football player, had gotten into the music business by working as a bodyguard for pop singer Bobby Brown. The two men struck up a friendship. When Knight learned that Dre was dissatisfied with Ruthless Records, he proposed a solution: the two could start a new record company together.

However, Dre was still under contract at Ruthless, meaning he could not work elsewhere. Somehow, Knight convinced Ruthless Records to let Dre out of his contract. According to some sources, Knight threatened Eazy-E with a baseball bat or a gun, although Knight has always denied that this happened. Whatever form of persuasion Knight used, Eazy-E allowed Dre to quit N.W.A and begin a solo career.

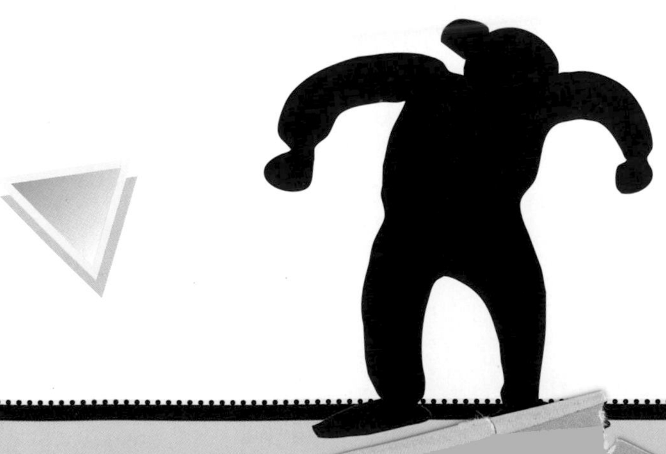

Dr. Dre emerged as a music superstar with the release of his debut album, *The Chronic*, in 1992. The influential album is widely considered a hip-hip masterpiece, and more than 4 million copies were sold.

4

Trouble at Death Row

Suge Knight and Dr. Dre named their new record label Death Row Records. They felt this name would leave little doubt about the type of music the label would produce: gangsta rap. The label's logo depicted a blindfolded black man strapped into an electric chair. It was a symbol for crime, violence, and hopelessness.

Knight was proud of his ties to the Bloods gang. He often wore red suits and had the walls of the company's offices painted red. Gang members were given jobs with the record company. "Death Row is a way of life," Knight told the *New York Times*. "It's an all-the-time thing. And ain't nobody gonna change that."

While Knight handled the business side of the company, Dre concentrated on the creative side. His first album for Death Row, *The Chronic*, was released in 1992. The name refers to a particularly potent strain of marijuana, and other songs on the album also glorified the use of drugs. While *The Chronic* contained familiar messages about crime, abuse of women, and violence, it showed greater lyrical sophistication than Dre's previous work. There were more complicated rhyme schemes, such as the one from "Nuthin' But a 'G' Thing":

> **"Well I'm peepin', and I'm creepin', and I'm creep-in'**
> **But I [nearly] got caught, 'cause my beeper kept beepin'**
> **Now it's time for me to make my impression felt**
> **So sit back, relax, and strap on your seatbelt**
> **You never been on a ride like this befo'**
> **Who can rap and control the maestro"**

The *New York Times* called *The Chronic* "the album that defined West Coast hip-hop. . . . It's the sound of a player enjoying ill-gotten gains but always watching his back. With its mixture of clarity and deep base punch, Dr. Dre's tracks jump out of ordinary car radios as well as boom-boxes and fancy sound systems."

To produce *The Chronic*, Dre employed sounds never heard before on hip-hop records. He brought in studio musicians to play saxophone and flute on the backgrounds of some of the tracks. He also utilized beats he drew from the type of funk and soul albums he played at his mother's parties. Fans responded by making *The Chronic* an overwhelming commercial success, earning Death Row more than $50 million in sales. The single "Nuthin' But a 'G' Thing" reached number two on the *Billboard* pop singles chart. Another hit, "Let Me Ride," won Dre the 1993 Grammy Award for Best Rap Solo Performance. The album was incredibly influential in the hip-hop music world, and many artists attempted to copy Dre's sound and production style.

The Chronic is notable for another reason. As with most of Dre's hip-hop albums, the record employed the talents of other rappers. Other than Dre, the rapper who contributed most to *The Chronic* was a young singer whom Dre had discovered in Compton. His name was Calvin Broadus, but he rapped under the name Snoop Doggy Dogg.

Snoop turned out to be a major talent for Death Row. Soon after *The Chronic* was released, Dre produced Snoop's first solo album, *Doggystyle*, which became one of the best-selling rap albums in history. "It ain't the Midas touch," Dre told *People* magazine shortly after

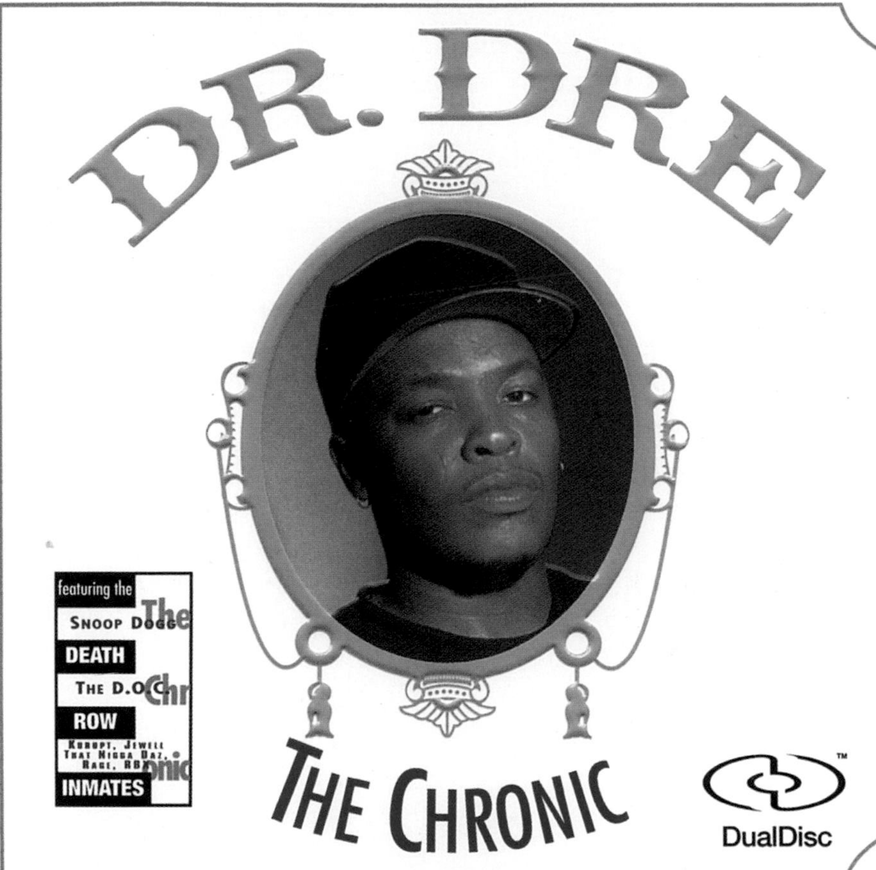

"Mixing loping beats, smooth and gruff voices from South Central, giggles, snarls and reggae . . . [*The Chronic's*] sounds are as raw and complex and real as life," commented a *Rolling Stone* reviewer. "This music . . . cannot be refuted or easily forgotten."

Doggystyle was released. "Midas only turned things into gold. I turn them into platinum."

Dre and Death Row were now enjoying unparalleled success in the hip-hop industry, but there was trouble on the horizon. Suge Knight had been feuding with an east coast rap producer named Sean "Puffy"

Combs, claiming that Combs's label produced a poor imitation of the West Coast gangsta sound. Their feud eventually led to what the press labeled the East Coast–West Coast rap war. For months, rappers for the two labels traded insults in the hip-hop press as well as on stage at concerts and award presentations. On August 3, 1995, at an awards

Death Row artists Tupac Shakur (left) and Snoop Dogg (center) pose with label cofounder Suge Knight for a promotional photo. *The Chronic* helped make Snoop Dogg into a major rap star. Dr. Dre produced Snoop's first solo album, *Doggystyle* (1993).

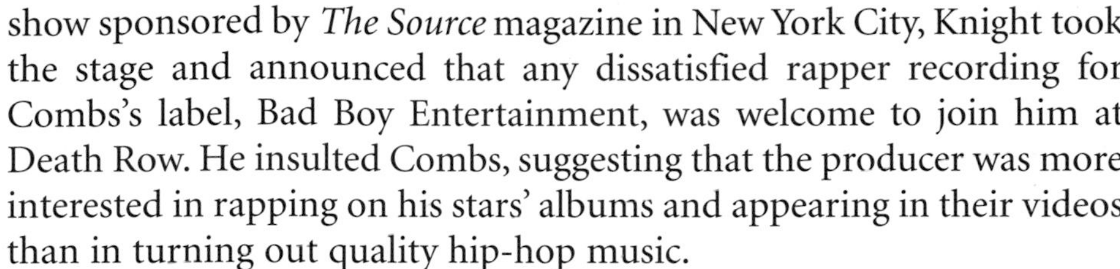

show sponsored by *The Source* magazine in New York City, Knight took the stage and announced that any dissatisfied rapper recording for Combs's label, Bad Boy Entertainment, was welcome to join him at Death Row. He insulted Combs, suggesting that the producer was more interested in rapping on his stars' albums and appearing in their videos than in turning out quality hip-hop music.

"Any artist out there that want to be an artist and want to stay a star and don't want to worry about the executive producer all up in the videos, all on the records—dancing, come to Death Row!" Knight proclaimed.

The New York audience grew hostile at Knight's insult. When Snoop Dogg took the stage a few minutes later he was greeted by a chorus of boos. "The East Coast ain't got no love for Dr. Dre and Snoop Doggy Dogg? And Death Row?" he asked. "*Ya'll don't love us?* Then let it be known that we got no love for the East Coast then!"

A Feud Becomes Violent

The war of words soon turned into a much different type of war. A month after the *Source* magazine awards show, rappers from the two feuding labels attended a birthday party in Atlanta, held in honor of So So Def Records founder Jermaine Dupri. Inevitably, the two sides clashed at the party. Shots were fired, and a Death Row employee named Jake Robles was killed. Knight immediately blamed Combs, but Combs claimed he had nothing to do with the altercation.

Tension between the two sides remained high. On September 7, 1996, violence in the rivalry erupted again when Death Row rapper Tupac Shakur was shot to death while sitting in a car on a street in Las Vegas, Nevada. No one is sure who was responsible for the rapper's shooting. The *Los Angeles Times* later published a series of articles suggesting that a Bad Boy rapper, the Notorious B.I.G., had ordered Tupac's murder, while *Rolling Stone* magazine published stories suggesting that it was Knight who ordered Tupac's murder because he owed the rapper some $3 million.

The feud flared up again the following spring. On March 9, 1997, the Notorious B.I.G. was shot to death while he sat in a car outside a party in Los Angeles. Knight again found himself under suspicion, as *Rolling Stone's* articles suggested the record **mogul** had ordered the slaying to deny Combs the services of his biggest star. Knight has denied the charge.

Bad Boy Records rapper Biggie Smalls—also known as Notorious B.I.G.—poses at the 1995 Billboard Music Awards. Dre tried to stay out of the feud between Bad Boy CEO Sean "Puffy" Combs and his Death Row partner, Suge Knight.

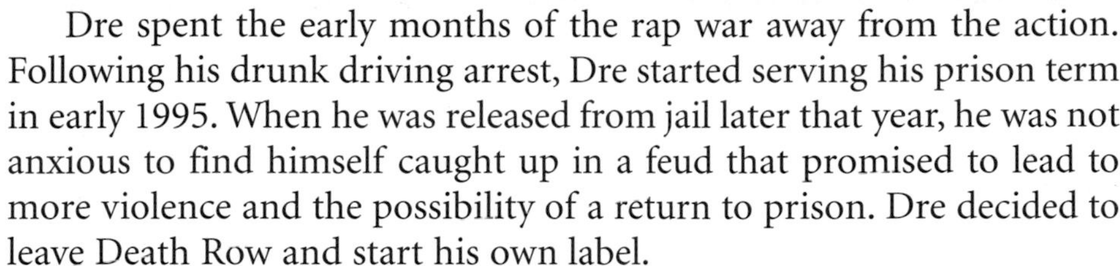

Dre spent the early months of the rap war away from the action. Following his drunk driving arrest, Dre started serving his prison term in early 1995. When he was released from jail later that year, he was not anxious to find himself caught up in a feud that promised to lead to more violence and the possibility of a return to prison. Dre decided to leave Death Row and start his own label.

Dre said that he did not like the direction in which Death Row Records was heading. He was also upset about the bad reputation that Knight had given the label by surrounding himself with thugs and gang members. "There was a lot of negative stuff going on there that had nothing to do with the music, and I wasn't comfortable with it," Dre told *Newsweek*. "I was the co-owner, and people—and I mean the wrong kind of people—were coming up to me on the street and saying, 'I'm on your label.'"

Dre's departure would not be a friendly parting of the ways. Knight refused to let Dre take his tapes with him—the dozens of unreleased recordings Dre produced remained at Death Row. Knight and several of the Death Row rappers, including Tupac before his death, publicly criticized Dre, calling him a traitor to the label. The producer was particularly stung to hear insults from Tupac, since Dre had performed with Tupac on the hit single "California Love" in 1996.

Dr. Dre holds the Legend Award he received at the 2000 Radio Music Awards program, the most prestigious prize given at the event. "It feels incredible," he later told reporters. "It's party time! I am only halfway through my career."

5

Back to His Roots

Dre named his new label Aftermath Entertainment, and quickly got down to the business of producing music. Early results were mixed. The label's first two releases were *Dr. Dre Presents . . . The Aftermath* (1996) and *The Firm: The Album* (1997). The records sold well, but critics suggested that the label's music was hardly cutting edge.

Dr. Dre Presents . . . The Aftermath featured tracks by several artists Dre had signed for his new label, along with tracks of his own. But critics found that his work as a rapper and producer was far superior to the other artists on the record. *Rolling Stone* critic Kevin Powell suggested that "beats have certainly made Dr. Dre's career, and the lack of them unmakes *Dre Presents . . . The Aftermath*." He added:

"Of the 16 tracks on the compilation, the only ones worth listening to feature Dr. Dre on the mike or behind

the boards. That's not to say Dre's new stable of artists isn't talented: Some of them, such as rapper Mel-Man, vocalist RC and the rhythm and blues female trio Hands-On, should do well when it's time for Dr. Dre to make an album for them. The problem is Dre's staff producers, Flossy P, Stu-B-Doo, Bud'da and Glove—they have the skills but just aren't on their boss's level yet."

Aftermath's other early release, *The Firm: The Album,* featured tracks by rappers Nas, Foxy Brown, AZ, and Nature. The album also received lukewarm reviews. Natasha Stovall of *Rolling Stone* wrote, "At their best, these MCs conjure a whole world and shoot it up with all the tragedy and comedy it can hold. But those stories also have a flip side: Often, the rappers' fantastic, blaxploitation-style adventures have all the spirit of an empty film canister."

True to His Art

Soon after leaving Death Row, Dre married his longtime girlfriend, Nicole, and bought a new home in California's San Fernando Valley. He stopped going to parties, instead coming home to be with their two children after working in the studio. Dre told reporters that he regarded himself as a family man and felt uncomfortable producing records laced with profanities. This was one reason *Dr. Dre Presents . . . The Aftermath* was different from his previous work. But after critics panned the album, Dre discussed the new direction with his wife. She told him to be true to his art. "My wife was like, yo, what are you doing?" Dre told *USA Today.* "She wanted to hear the hardcore. She still has *The Chronic* in the CD player in her car. So I was like, let me get back to being me."

In 1999, Dre produced a follow-up to *The Chronic* titled *Dr. Dre 2001,* in which the rapper returned to his roots. This album was welcomed by his fans and critics. One of the songs on *Dr. Dre 2001* was titled "Still Dre." It included the lyrics:

"[M]y last album was *The Chronic*
They want to know if he still got it
They say rap's changed, they want to know how
I feel about it . . .

Dre married his longtime girlfriend, Nicole Young, in May 1995, shortly after he left Death Row. In this 2002 photo, the couple arrives at the Los Angeles premiere of rapper Eminem's hit movie *8 Mile*.

Dr. Dre is the name, I'm ahead of my game
Still, puffing my leafs, still with the beats
Still not loving police (Uh huh)
Still rock my khakis with a cuff and a crease
Still got love for the streets . . .
Still the beat bangs, still doing my thang
Since I left, ain't too much changed. . . .''

To help make the album a success, Dre used a lot of the same talent he employed to produce *The Chronic*, including Snoop Dogg. In producing the album, Dre did little **sampling**. Instead, he hired musicians to create original sounds. He used a lot of experimental sounds on the album, such as guitars, a piano, a Moog synthesizer, and even a ukulele. "I don't think it's possible for hip-hop to grow if producers just keep copying what has already been done," Dre told *Keyboard*. "I use those old records simply as motivation, but I try to stay away from sampling. There are times I might use it, but I'm not going to base a whole album around someone else's music."

Village Voice music critic Raquel Cepeda wrote that in producing *Dr. Dre 2001*, Dre is "on top of his game," adding that "*2001* is the kind of record that . . . raises the bar exam for producers from now until Dre's next [record]."

Dre's reputation as the top rap producer in the country was solidified when he signed Eminem and produced the rapper's two dynamic records, *The Slim Shady LP* (1999) and *The Marshall Mathers LP* (2000).

Acting Opportunities

In 2001, Dre added acting to his list of career accomplishments by appearing in two movies. One film was a gritty drama that exposed the underbelly of police corruption in Los Angeles; the other was a lighthearted comedy.

The comedy was *The Wash*, which featured Dre and Snoop Dogg in the lead roles. Dre plays Sean, the manager of a car wash while Snoop portrays Dee Loc, one of his employees who uses the car wash to carry out his shady street deals. The film had a brief run in theaters and then disappeared quickly.

The police drama turned out to be one of the major film releases of 2001. Titled *Training Day*, the movie told the story of a group of crooked Los Angeles police officers who operate a drug-dealing ring.

Dr. Dre and Snoop Dogg are featured on the cover of *Blaze* magazine. The two rappers teamed up again on Dre's highly successful follow-up to *The Chronic, Dr.Dre 2001*. The album was praised by critics and sold more than 6 million copies.

The ring was headed by Detective Alonzo Harris, played by Denzel Washington, who won an Academy Award for his portrayal of the **rogue** cop. Dre played the role of Paul, a policeman who followed Alonzo's lead and helped him kill another cop who wanted to break up the ring. The movie was filmed on location in such Los Angeles neighborhoods as Imperial Courts and Crenshaw, which were similar to the crime-infested neighborhood in Compton where Dre grew up.

"I was impressed that the production went to the real places where these things really go down," Dre said. "They went to Imperial Courts, to the Jungle, to Crenshaw, and they weren't afraid of getting dirty.

Eminem (left) and Dre (right) discovered the unknown rapper 50 Cent and agreed to jointly produce his first album. 50 Cent's debut, *Get Rich or Die Tryin'*, was a smash success that reached number one Billboard magazine's album chart.

[Director] Antoine Fuqua told me he was taking the gloves off to shoot this movie, and he meant it."

Snoop Dogg had a small part in *Training Day* as well, playing a crippled hoodlum confined to a wheelchair. Said screenwriter David Ayer, "I think the supporting cast adds a lot of spice to the movie. Snoop is hilarious—he just clicks; Dr. Dre is fantastic in action, the kind of guy you would never want to mess with."

Finding 50 Cent

While Dre was spending time on movie sets, his **protégé** Eminem, was carving himself out a place as a major hip-hop star. Eminem was not only a talented rapper, but he had an eye for other talent as well. In 2002, a young rapper named Curtis James Jackson III caught Eminem's attention. Eminem approached Dre and proposed they form a partnership to sign Jackson, who performed under the name 50 Cent, and produce his first album. Dre agreed, and the two rap stars reportedly paid more than $1 million to sign 50 Cent.

The money was worth it. In 2003, Aftermath and Eminem's own record label, Shady Records, jointly released 50 Cent's album *Get Rich or Die Tryin'*. It became a runaway hit, selling nearly a million copies in its first week of release. Critics recognized 50 Cent's talent, but they also gave credit to Dre and Eminem for crafting the album. Wrote *Newsday* music critic Glenn Gamboa, "Dr. Dre co-writes four tracks and produces three more, and his style dominates the project: loads of spare, yet ominous, synths and simple rhythm tracks."

Although some are jealous of Dr. Dre's success, most people involved in the hip-hop world recognize and respect his talent and creativity. Over the years, he has received many awards for his major contributions to hip-hop music.

6

A Gangsta's Dangerous World

Despite success as a rap star and producer, Dr. Dre knows how difficult it is to leave the gangsta life behind. While attending the 2004 *Vibe* Awards show in California, where he was given the Legend Award, Dre was approached by a man asking for his autograph. The man then unexpectedly lashed out and punched Dre.

The punch thrown by Jimmy James Johnson sparked a brawl that led to mayhem at the awards program. Hundreds of people, including some of the top names in the music business, were caught up in the **melee** near the stage. Members of the rap group G-Unit, including 50 Cent, Young Buck, Lloyd Bands, and Tony Yayo, jumped in to protect Dre. They were reportedly throwing both punches and chairs. The police had to spray mace to break up the brawl. Jimmy Henchman, a producer of the awards program, told MTV News:

> **“Dre, being the gentleman that he is, was about to sign the autograph when the guy punched him. It was nothing, though. Dre handled him. Dre grabbed the dude and handled him. You could tell somebody put a battery in the kid's back to do what he did. He jumped out there.”**

In the scuffle, Johnson broke away from Dre and was swallowed up by the crowd. During the pushing and shoving that ensued, Johnson sustained a stab wound. Soon after the awards program, a young rapper named Young Buck, was arrested and charged with attempted murder for stabbing Johnson. The charge was later reduced to assault when it was learned that Johnson had been stabbed with a fork. Young Buck was able to stay out of prison by accepting a sentence of community service—he would have to spend several hours serving on a highway cleanup crew or doing similar labor.

As for the original **assailant**, Jimmy James Johnson, he recovered from his wound but was sentenced to a year in jail. Eventually, Johnson told reporters that Suge Knight—evidently still angry with Dre over their falling-out—had paid him to punch Dre. Said Henchman, “Suge was there, you had a few other characters that were there from Los Angeles, Snoop was there, Dre was there. . . . Some people felt a little uncomfortable, people who knew the history.”

Knight denied paying Johnson to punch his former partner. “One thing about me, if I do something, I claim it,” Knight insisted to reporters following the awards show. “I'm not an idiot. See, an idiot would go out there and do stuff.”

As for Dr. Dre, once the mayhem died down, he did make it onto the stage to accept the Legend Award. “They can't stop me, I don't care,” said Dre as he accepted the award. The awards show was reconvened the following day so the rest of the event could be taped. The brawl was edited out of the aired version. Nevertheless, the incident at the *Vibe* Awards show served as a grim reminder to those in attendance that hip-hop remains a dangerous world. Jimmy Henchman told reporters later:

Rapper Young Buck (center, wearing black hat) was arrested and accused of stabbing Jimmy James Johnson during the *Vibe* awards show brawl. He was later sentenced to three years probation and 80 hours of community service for his role in the fight.

"It hurts us, hurts hip-hop, hurts the whole experience. It's just a shame that there is no real forum for us to enjoy ourselves. You had the [American Music Awards] one night prior that went eventless, then you had the *Vibe* Awards. When they punched Dre, they punched the whole industry in the face."

Hip-Hop has a Heart

In recent years, Americans suffered from two horrific tragedies—the 2001 terrorist attacks on the World Trade Center in New York City and the Pentagon near Washington, D.C., and the 2005 devastation caused when Hurricane Katrina swept through New Orleans and other Gulf Coast cities. In both cases, Dr. Dre offered his help.

Two weeks after the terrorist attacks, a number of celebrities from the entertainment community staged "Stand Up for New York," a **telethon** to raise money for the families of the 3,000 victims of the terrorist attacks. Entertainers Tom Hanks, Jerry Seinfeld, Diana Ross, Bono, Michael Jackson, Whitney Houston, Paul McCartney, Rosie O'Donnell, Sandra Bullock, Jim Carrey, and Julia Roberts all contributed. Dr. Dre led the hip-hop community in the effort, donating $1 million to the fund to aid the families.

Four years later, Americans were called on to help the victims of Hurricane Katrina. Thousands of people were left homeless by the storm that flooded New Orleans and other cities. Again, Dr. Dre contributed $1 million. This time, his aid went to the Julia C. Hester

In October 2005, Dr. Dre donated $1 million to help families who were impacted by Hurricane Katrina. In this photo from the ceremony at the Julia C. Hester House in Houston, two women from New Orleans hug after learning they would receive a $20,000 gift from Dre.

House, an organization in Houston that selected 50 families to help rebuild their lives after the storm. Each family received $20,000 through Dre's gift. Dre told the Associated Press, "I wanted to be sure that my donation did two things: went directly into the hands of hurricane victims and that it was an amount of cash that could really impact their lives and make a difference." Dre chose Hester House because the organization was willing to give 100 percent of the donation to those who needed it.

Guiding Young Talent

As a performer, Dre planned to release his next CD in 2006. The album's release date has been changed several times, and Dre had even told reporters that he had given the project up. However, current rumors are that he is still working on it. Titled *Detox*, the album will tell the story of a killer for hire who questions the direction his life has taken. Unlike most hip-hop albums, which include a group of songs that may have a loose association to one another, each song on *Detox* is expected to tell a different part of the story of the killer's life. Dre told MTV News:

> **"I had to come up with something different but still keep it hardcore, so what I decided to do was make my album one story about one person and just do the record through a character's eyes. And everybody that appears on my album is going to be a character, so it's basically going to be a hip-hop musical."**

For the most part, though, Dre prefers the role of producer. He has found that he can be much more of an influence on hip-hop music by discovering new talent, molding the sounds of rising hip-hop stars, and producing their records. After honing the careers of Snoop Dogg, Eminem, and 50 Cent, he is now producing records for The Game, a rapper from Compton who has been hailed by critics as hip-hop's next big star. When The Game's first album, *The Documentary*, was released in 2005 it quickly went platinum and hit the top of the hip-hop charts. In an interview with *Scratch* magazine, hip-hop producer and record company executive Just Blaze called *The Documentary* the best-produced album of 2005. Blaze said he sat in on some of the recording sessions and was awed by Dre's work on the album. Said Blaze, "He was there every day. Whether it was his record or not. That just shows you that when he wants to go in on something hard look at the end result. It's the best put-together album of the year."

Dre's reputation as hip-hop's top producer has prompted recording artists from other genres to approach him about producing their albums. For example, the pop singer Madonna once asked Dre to produce an album, but he refused. "I have no interest in working with Madonna," Dre told *People* magazine. "I like building an artist and watching him sign his first autograph. That's my kick. New acts don't have egos."

Today, Dre is concentrating on signing and developing new talent for Aftermath Entertainment. One of his biggest current stars is rapper The Game, whose debut album *The Documentary* (2005) sold more than a million copies.

"Although I'm from the West Coast, I try to make music that will have a universal appeal," Dre wrote on his Web site in 2001. "It's always been my desire to make music for the world."

According to rap star Kanye West, "He's the definition of a true talent: Dre feels like God placed him here to make music, and no matter what forces are aligned against him, he always ends up on the mountaintop."

1965 Andre Young born in Compton, California, on February 18.

1986 Dre joins four other rappers to form the hip-hop group N.W.A.

1989 N.W.A's second album, *Straight Outta Compton*, soars to the top of the hip-hop charts and causes a national furor for advocating violence against the police.

1991 *Efil4zaggin* is released by N.W.A. Dre quits N.W.A and founds Death Row Records with Marion "Suge" Knight. Dre is charged with assaulting a TV host in a nightclub; he is sentenced to house arrest.

1992 Dre charged with assaulting a New Orleans police officer and is again placed on house arrest; *The Chronic*, Dre's first album for Death Row Records, is released. Dre punches a record producer and is sentenced to house arrest.

1994 Dre arrested for drunken driving and, because he violated his probation on the 1992 assault charge, is sentenced to five months in prison, which he begins serving in 1995.

1995 The East Coast–West Coast feud heats up when Knight insults rival record producer Sean "Puffy" Combs at the *Source* magazine awards show. After his release from prison, Dre vows to stay out of trouble with the law. He leaves Death Row and starts his own label, Aftermath Entertainment.

1996 Death Row rapper Tupac Shakur is murdered in a drive-by shooting in September.

1997 The Notorious B.I.G., who records for Combs's Bad Boy Entertainment label, is murdered in a drive-by shooting in March.

1998 After hearing a demo tape made by Eminem, Dre signs the young rapper to a record contract.

1999 Dre releases *Dr. Dre 2001*, which receives good reviews because it reflects Dre's return to his gangsta roots.

2001 *The Marshall Mathers LP*, produced by Dre, is nominated for a Grammy Award as Album of the Year; Dre acts in two films, *The Wash* and *Training Day*; donates $1 million to aid the victims of the September 11 terrorist attacks.

2002 Dre and Eminem sign rapper 50 Cent to a record contract and produce his first album, *Get Rich or Die Tryin'*.

2004 Dre is assaulted by a fan at the *Vibe* Awards, where he is presented the magazine's Legend Award; later, it is alleged the assailant was paid by Suge Knight to punch Dre. Knight denies the charge.

2005 Dre produces *The Documentary*, the debut album for rapper The Game that soars to the top of the hip-hop charts. Dre donates $1 million to aid the victims of Hurricane Katrina.

2006 Dr. Dre's long-delayed album *Detox* scheduled for release at the end of the year.

Discography

Albums with N.W.A

1987 *N.W.A and the Posse*

1988 *Straight Outta Compton*

1990 *100 Miles and Runnin'*

1991 *Efil4zaggin*

Solo Albums

1992 *The Chronic*

1994 *Concrete Roots*

1996 *Greatest Hits*
Dr. Dre Presents . . . The Aftermath
First Round Knock Out
Back 'N the Day

1999 *Dr. Dre 2001*

2001 *Maximum Dr. Dre*

2002 *Chronicle: Best of the Work*

2004 *Greatest Hits V.2*

Film

2001 *The Wash*
Training Day

Awards

1994 Winner, American Music Awards for Favorite Rap-Hip Hop Artist and Favorite New Rap-Hip Hop Artist.

Winner, Grammy Award for Best Rap Solo Performance for "Let Me Ride" and nominated for Best Rap Performance by a Duo or Group with Snoop Dogg for "Nuthin' But a 'G' Thing."

Winner, *Source* Awards for Solo Artist of the Year, Album of the Year, and Producer of the Year.

1996 Nominated for a Grammy Award for Best Rap Solo Performance for "Keep Their Heads Ringin'."

Nominated with Tupac Shakur for an MTV Video Music Award for Best Rap Video for "California Love."

1997 Nominated with Tupac Shakur for a Grammy Award for Best Rap Performance by a Duo or Group for "California Love."

2000 Winner, MTV Video Music Award for Best Rap Video for "Forget About Dre" and nominated for Best Director for Eminem's "The Real Slim Shady."

2001 Winner, Grammy Awards for Best Rap Performance by a Duo or Group for "Forget About Dre" with Eminem, and Best Rap Album for *The Marshall Mathers LP*; nominated for Album of the Year for *The Marshall Mathers LP*.

2002 Nominated for Grammy Awards for Producer of the Year and Best Music Video for Missy Elliott's "Knoc."

2004 Received Legend Award from *Vibe* magazine.

2006 Nominated for a Grammy Award for Best Rap Performance by a Duo or Group for "Encore" with Eminem and 50 Cent.

Castro, Peter. "The Doctor Is In." *People Weekly* 41, no. 19 (May 3, 1999), p. 63–66.

Duralde, Alonso. "The Trouble with Eminem." *The Advocate* no. 832 (February 27, 2001), p. 57.

Gold, Jonathan. "Day of the Dre." *Rolling Stone* no. 666 (September 30, 1993), p. 38–42.

Griffin, Verna. *Privileged to Live: A Mother's Story of Survival.* Los Angeles: Milligan Books, 2005.

Kenyatta, Kelly. *You Forgot About Dre: The Unauthorized Biography of Dr. Dre and Eminem.* Chicago: Busta Books, 2000.

Krough, John. "Dr. Dre: Back After All These Years." *Keyboard* 26, no. 3 (March 2001), p. 14.

Ogg, Alex, and David Upshal. *The Hip Hop Years: A History of Rap*. New York: Fromm International, 2001.

Pareles, Jon. "Outlaw Rock: More Skirmishes on the Censorship Front." *New York Times* (December 10, 1989), p. A-32.

Reibman, Greg. "Anti-Obscenity Lawyer Looks to Get Rap Group N.W.A Banned in Boston." *Boston Herald* (August 9, 1991), p. S-21.

Watkins, S. Craig. *Hip Hop Mattters: Politics, Pop Culture, and the Struggle for the Soul of a Movement.* Boston: Beacon Press, 2005.

Web Sites

www.aftermath-entertainment.com
The Web site for Dr. Dre's Aftermath Entertainment.

www.comptoncity.org/index.html
Web site maintained by the city government of Compton, California.

www.deathrowrecords.net
Web site for Tha Row (formerly known as Death Row Records).

www.dre2001.com
Dr. Dre's official Web site.

http://foia.fbi.gov/foiaindex/cripsbloods.htm
An archive of newspaper and magazine stories on the Crips and Bloods.

http://www.vh1.com/artists/interview/1455173/06132002/dr_dre.jhtml
Dr. Dre talks about his discovery of rapper Eminem.

assailant—a person who initiates an attack.

electro hop—a form of dance/hip-hop music that developed on the West Coast.

genre—a category of artistic expression. Music includes numerous genres, such as hip-hop, rock 'n' roll, pop, jazz, and classical.

ghetto—depressed area of an inner city where poor people live because they lack the means to move out.

gig—a performance that an entertainer is paid to give before an audience.

lyrics—words to a song.

melee—large and confusing fight in which many people participate.

mogul—powerful corporate executive who dominates an industry.

music mixer—a device that allows a user to merge the music from multiple sources into a single stream of sound.

obscenity—word or action that offends the moral standards of the community.

probation—status granted to a criminal that permits him or her supervised freedom outside jail.

protégé—young person whose career is guided by someone with more knowledge and experience.

rogue—dishonest person, often working secretly for evil purposes.

sampling—taking a short musical phrase from one song and using it in another recording.

telethon—televised production staged to raise money for a worthy cause; viewers at home are asked to phone in promises to donate.

triple platinum—RIAA certification signifying three million records sold.

turntable—a record player.

urban—relating to life in a city.

Hal Marcovitz is a journalist who has written more than 70 books for young readers as well as the satirical novel *Painting the White House.* His other biographies in the HIP-HOP series include *Notorious B.I.G.* and *Tupac.* He lives in Chalfont, Pennsylvania, with his wife, Gail, and daughters Ashley and Michelle.

Picture Credits

page

2: Rosa Williams/Famous/ ACE Pictures
8: Zuma Press/Ken Weingart
11: Zuma Press/Nancy Kaszerman
13: KRT/Nancy Stone
14: AFP Photo/Hector Mata
16: Zuma Press/Ken Weingart
19: NMI/Michelle Feng
21: KRT/David Leeson
22: NMI/Michelle Feng
24: ZUMA Archive
27: NMI/Michelle Feng
29: Zuma Press/Ken Weingart
30: KRT/Chuck Fadely
32: ZUMA Archive
35: NMI/Michelle Feng
36: Death Row Records/NMI
38: Zuma Press/Jane Caine
40: Zuma Press/Lisa O'Connor
43: Tsuni/iPhoto
45: Business Wire photo/NMI
46: Dara Kushner/INFGoff
48: KRT/Lionel Hahn
51: David Claborn/Splash News
52: AP Photo/Donna Carson
54: INFGoff/kguk-03
55: PRNewsFoto/NMI

Front cover: ZUMA Archive
Back cover: © Roger Miller/Corbis